It's About the **"Boys"**

...Getting from Boyhood-to-Manhood

Written by Patrice Lee

Illustrated by Francesco Paolo Ardizzone

It's About the **"Boys"**
Copyright, 2018
Printed in the United States of America
Published by Leep4Joy Books, a Division of Feinstein Development

All rights reserved. No part of this book may be reproduced, copied or transmitted in any form/by any means without written consent from the author.

Publisher's Cataloging-In-Publication Data
(Prepared by The Donohue Group, Inc.)

Names: Lee, Patrice. | Ardizzone, Francesco Paolo, illustrator.
Title: It's about the "boys" : ... getting from boyhood-to-manhood / written by Patrice Lee ; illustrated by Francesco Paolo Ardizzone.
Other Titles: It is about the "boys" : ... getting from boyhood-to-manhood
Description: Oak Park, MI : Leep4Joy Books, a division of Feinstein & Associates, [2018] | Interest grade level: PreK-4. | Summary: A book that helps boys realize that they really are okay just being boys. Also, a book for parents and teachers to help them understand how boys think.
Identifiers: ISBN 9780986316777
Subjects: LCSH: Boys--Psychology--Juvenile fiction. | Boys--Conduct of life--Juvenile fiction. | Masculinity--Psychological aspects--Juvenile fiction. | Self-esteem in children--Juvenile fiction. | CYAC: Boys--Psychology--Fiction. | Boys--Conduct of life--Fiction. | Masculinity--Psychological aspects--Fiction. | Self-esteem--Fiction.
Classification: LCC PZ7.1.L44 It 2018 | DDC [E]--dc23

Edited by: Chelynne Lee
Children's Book Consultant: Stephen Moore
Illustrated by: Francesco Paolo Ardizzone
Title Word Placement-Cover; Page Layout: Bob Ivory Jr., IvoryCoast Media

Please send all correspondence to: PatriceALee@gmail.com or
Feinstein and Associates, P.O. Box 48172, Oak Park, MI 48237

Dedicated to:

Sons and **"boys"** who need us to understand that it's not an easy road to becoming a young man. And to the moms who kept asking me, "Do you have a book for little boys?" Mom{s}, this one is for you, and the "**boys**."

Acknowledgement

Heavenly Father: Thank You for your infinite wisdom, and for placing the gift of writing within me. I desire to please You, as I use my gift to help others.

Allen Einstein: I'm so thankful I attended the Left/Right Brain Differences of Boys and Girls workshop, and have applied what I learned on addressing certain left-brain behaviors in this book.

Francesco P. Ardizzone: Your illustrated art is superb! Many, many thanks!

Bobby Ivory, Jr., Chelynne Lee, and Stephen Moore: Thank you for your thoughtful attention to details. It's About the **"Boys!"** is a much better book because of you.

Introduction

It's About the **"Boys"** is a great read for boys because they can identify with the characters in the book, who demonstrate that it's okay to be a {busy, fidgety, boisterous} "boy."

It's About the **"BOYS!"** is creatively narrated by **boys**, Danny and Kenny, who share what's best for their left-brain way of thinking and a healthy life, on their journey from boyhood-to-manhood.

You will see how much these two boys from different ethnic groups have in common. They stay busy, in a good way, as they enjoy living life.

Although this book includes helpful information for moms and educators, it really is for, and about, the **"boys."** As we apply the information shared, our community will reap the benefits too.

.

I present to you: *It's About the* **"Boys"**

"Main Characters"

Hi! I'm Danny, narrator, main character, and one of the **"boys."**

This is my Mom. She encourages my sister, my Dad and me. Of all the moms in the world, she is the absolute best that a mom can be.

Here's my Dad. He's happy and whistles a lot. He teaches me things like how to 'tie-a-tie,' and how to make a knot.

My sister: Onya ☺

This is my friend, Kenny, co-narrator; also, one of the **"boys."**

Kenny's sister

It's "Love – Unconditional"

When I was born there was so much "joy"
For it was God who decided, 'we need another boy.'
For in Him, and in everything He makes
Everything is good. There are no mistakes.

It was "love" that brought me here. I know.
But, it's "love - unconditional" that helps me grow.
And as I mature, you'll begin to understand, that
"Love – unconditional" will help me become a man.

~

"Unconditional love" – sees past my imperfections, and encourages me along the way. "Unconditional love" helps me strive for excellence each day.

My name is Danny Fishback. I play games and sports activities.
I do a lot of things outside. I have a skateboard, "neon" scooter,
And a bicycle I like to ride. They say I have wisdom beyond my years;
That my thoughts are very deep. Though I'm good-natured, I'm quiet.
You'll seldom hear me speak.

My sister, on the other hand, is dainty, kind, and sweet.
The clothes she wears always nice and neat.
My sister speaks very well. She's quite ar-ti-cu-late. For she talks to Mom about everything, from science to baking chocolate.

But, when dad and I do things together, we don't say a lot.
We enjoy each other's company, but, we don't talk half as much.
I'm not at all concerned about my clothes and stuff.
I love the outdoors. In fact, I play very rough.

I may not have a lot say, but teachers think I'm smart;
For I excel in math and science, technology, and art.
My "brain," they say, is "still developing." {That's adult talk!}
I'm not sure what it means. I'm just glad
They're sayin' 'good things' when they speak of me.

{Next Page}

And, I like when the teacher sends me on errands at school,
I get to walk through the hallways without breaking any rules.
I get to do something different and feel important too!
Most of all, it lets me know that they trust me, and that's cool.

Now when something's really bothering me,
Those feelings deep inside of me are something I cannot hide.
That's when Dad and I go for a "little walk," or a very "leisurely ride."
The fresh air does wonders for me, …helps me open up and talk.

I'm Kenny McAbee. I also have a sister,
Who's not at all like me. Though, we get along together,
We seldom think alike. I think mostly from my "<u>left brain</u>."
She thinks (mostly) from the "<u>right</u>."

The two of us are as different as the "day is from the night."
But, we get along together, 'cause we choose to help each other,
Not to fuss or fight. I look out for her, and she looks out for me.
We have love for one another. We are family.

Now that you've met my sister, I'll tell you more about me.
I wake up early in the morning. It doesn't matter what time.
I just wake up - "happy" – I'm happy all o' the time.
And when I get up, I do a stretch or two.
I give thanks for my family, and for my loved ones too.
I ask for guidance through each day, and of course, I pray for you.

In summer months, I spend time climbing trees and having loads of fun.
The grown-ups say fresh air is good for us, that we need a little sun.
For it gives the vitamin D we need, to strengthen bones and teeth.

But, if you want to know what's on our mind,
You may have to wait awhile; because our brain's are busy
"Thinking-and-reasoning" behind these great big smiles. ☺

If you ever need us, we'll be there to lend a hand.
But, no matter how you feel about us, it helps if you understand,
We're **"boys!!!"** . . .and, as a *young* **"boy**," I'm still developing into
A "respectable and responsible" man.

Prayer of Gratitude

Dear Heavenly Father,

I know You have a special plan for me;
For You gave your only "Son" Jesus, to die at Calvary.

As a son, I believe You understand me when no one else can. I invite YOU into my heart Lord Jesus, so I can spend more time with You. Please forgive me for the times I've sinned, and disappointed You. Thank you for your love, for hearing my prayers, and answering them too.

Today I put my trust in You. Thank You for letting me be your son too. Now, 24/7, I can talk to You.

Love,

_____

(Your name)

Poems -

About the **"Boys"**

Just **"Us"** Boys

Just "Us" Boys

The two of "us" boys are 8 years old. We come from two loving families.

Though unique, we have some commonalities. We live in the same vicinity, . . .are connected to the (same) community.

We're of a specific ethnicity, and sometimes see things differently,

~

M.A.L.E.

"M" is for mindset. I think more than I speak. But, whenever I communicate, I'm sharp on my feet.

"A" is for active. I like to keep busy.' Please don't ask me to be (sit) still.

"L" is for loud and boisterous. I like to keep it real. Then there's an

"E" for energetic. I need to move around. With so much energy to burn, I just can't sit down.

Male - *opposite of female; a gender of, or related to a man*

Reference: ". . .God created man in His own image, in the image of God created He him; male and female created he them" (Genesis 1:27).

I Need **You** To Understand - *"Me!"*

Sometimes I need you to understand me, for who I am right now,
For you know not where I'm going, and who I want to be.

Sometimes I need to be alone – there in my own space
Where I have time to think or move at a slower pace.

For where I'm headed I haven't been before.
So I need this time to take in new thoughts, and the time to explore.

For each day is filled with opportunity, bustling with activity.
And I am full of hope as I expand my capacity …to learn me.

Growing into the respectable, responsible man you want me to be,
I'm preparing for my tomorrow – to live out my destiny.

Movin' from "*Boy*hood...to Manhood"

Please don't expect **me** to be still. For I
Need you to understand ...that I'm a boy ...still growing.
I'm not a grown man.
I run. I jump. I play ball.
Didn't you see me climb that wall?
That's because I'm a boy . . .I'm still growing.
. . .And I need you to understand.
I've got energy to burn, and much to learn. And I'm still **growing!**
So please understand
That I'm movin' from *boy*hood into manhood,
But, for now - I'm just a **boy** who's **still grow-ing!**
. . .soon to be a man.

Developmental Differences of "Boys" and Girls

Just some things you need to know to be a better communicator with the boys.

Parent Note: Throughout various stages of development, there are notable differences between males and females, beginning with early childhood. Here's a list of some of those differences.

"Boy" Facts:

Pre-Birth:	Brain produces less serotonin (has a calming effect)
Infant:	Sensitive to salty foods; less bothered by loud noise
At 3 years:	A greater muscle mass is already evident
Pre-K:*	More active; rough; competitive; aggressive
Grades 1-3:	Better in math; make up 95% of hyperactive children

Girl Facts:

Pre-Birth:	Brain produces more serotonin (has a calming effect)
Infants:	Sensitive to bitter tastes and loud noise; prefers sweets
At 3 yrs:	Greater concentration of fatty tissue than muscle mass
Pre-K:*	Play quietly; less physical; expresses emotions thru words
Grades 1-3:	Better w/verbal skills; make up 5% of hyperactive children

* Pre-K - {Pre-School – Kindergarten}

The Mind of Boys–Saving Our Sons from Falling Behind in School and Life by Michael Gurian.

Epilogue

It's important that children have a healthy, balanced life. The balance is a little more difficult to achieve when the dad is not involved in his child's life. It tougher on the "**boys**," because boys need someone to emulate, and God didn't mean for moms do the job alone. With so many boys being raised in fatherless homes, many moms welcome support to help their sons realize their potential for greatness. This book serves as a support and a resource for learning.

<u>For *the* "**boys:**"</u> It's a great read for boys because they can identify with the characters in the book, and it reinforces that it's really okay, to be a {busy, fidgety, boisterous} boy. More than anything I want *the* "**boys**" to enjoy this book, because they need to know that they are "special" in a good way. ☺

<u>For Moms/teachers</u>: This book highlights boys' left-brain thinking, and demonstrates ways to increase productivity in, and out of the classroom. As you read to your sons/students, and apply the many energy-channeling solutions from the examples provided you will reap the benefits.

Please note the value placed on the role of a father in Proverbs:

"Hear, ye children, the instruction of a father, and attend to know understanding" {Prov. 4:1}.
"My son, hear the instruction of thy father, and forsake not the law of thy mother" {Proverbs 1:8}

New Words: Definitions, sentences, and more. . .

1. On a separate sheet of paper, list the words below in alphabetical order.
2. Using a dictionary, look up each word and write the definition.
3. Construct a complete sentence for each word.
4. Please underline the new word in each sentence.

<u>Example</u>:

Articulate - to speak or express oneself with precision; without error
He is quite <u>articulate</u> with his words.

"Boy" – the male offspring of man and woman, created by God.

Integrity

Respectable

Responsible

Energetic

Boisterous - sometimes loud; sometimes noisy, rough; without restraint

Opportunity

Destiny

Vicinity

Capacity

Maturity

Ethnicity

Exceptional

5. What do you want to be when you grow up? Why?

_____

_____

6. How will you make the world a better place? Explain.

_____

_____

7. Do you have a hobby? Tell us about your hobby.

_____

_____

8. What makes you happy?

_____

9. What activities do you like to do with your family?

_____

_____

10. If you could make only one change in the world to make it a better place, what would you change?

_____

_____

Want another Leep4Joy Book?

Go to: www.Leep4Joy.com

See our list of Reader's Favorite 5-star books below:

Happy To Be Me!
https://www.createspace.com/4680003

Happy To Be Me! Coloring Book
https://www.createspace.com/7246621

The Bully Met My Dad! …and Became My Friend
https://www.createspace.com/5083044

Let's **"Love"** One Another
https://www.createspace.com/5844394

Let's **"Love"** One Another Coloring Book
https://www.createspace.com/7233385

It's Just a "CIRCUMSTANCE"
https://www.createspace.com/6896487

Adult/Teen Best Seller:
How To Overcome Every Obstacle and Land on Top
https://www.createspace.com/3884601

Bully Me?...Oh No!!! …Suicide is not an Option
https://www.createspace.com/4082811

If you like our books please let us know: PatriceALee@gmail.com
Twitter: @Leep4Joy
FaceBook: Leep4Joy Books

Made in the USA
Lexington, KY
25 November 2019